OCS Report
MMS 2002-076

Investigation of Fatal Rental Crane Support Brace Failure
Main Pass Block 255 "A" Platform
OCS-G 07825
May 5, 2002

Gulf of Mexico
Off the Louisiana Coast

U.S. Department of the Interior
Minerals Management Service
Gulf of Mexico OCS Regional Office

OCS Report
MMS 2002-076

Investigation of Fatal Rental Crane Support Brace Failure Main Pass Block 255 "A" Platform OCS-G 07825 May 5, 2002

Gulf of Mexico
Off the Louisiana Coast

Jack Williams, Chair
Tom Machado
Stephen P. Dessauer

U.S. Department of the Interior
Minerals Management Service
Gulf of Mexico OCS Regional Office

New Orleans
December 2002

Contents

Investigation and Report

Authority
On Sunday, 5 May 2002, construction operations were underway to install a new flare boom and to remove the old, 18,000-lb flare boom from Devon's "A" platform in Main Pass Block 255. The old flare boom was to be cut from the platform's north side and lowered onto a work boat by using a temporarily installed rental crane. After the flare boom was cut free, and while the load was being swung around the northeast corner of the platform, one of the crane's two support braces failed, causing the crane suddenly to break free and be pulled overboard into the Gulf of Mexico. The movement of the crane overboard caused the death of one of the crew members who was in the path of the falling crane.

The event occurred 5 May 2002 at approximately 0800 hrs on the Operator's lease, OCS-G 07825, Main Pass Block 255 in the Gulf of Mexico, offshore the State of Louisiana.

Pursuant to Section 208, Subsection 22 (d), (e), and (f), of the Outer Continental Shelf (OCS) Lands Act, as amended in 1978, and the Department of the Interior Regulations 30 CFR 250, the Minerals Management Service (MMS) is required to investigate and prepare a public report of this accident. By memorandum dated 10 May 2002, the following MMS personnel were named to the investigative panel:

Jack Williams, Chairman – Office of Safety Management, Field Operations, GOM OCS Region;

Tom Machado - New Orleans District, Field Operations, GOM OCS Region;

Stephen P. Dessauer - New Orleans District, Field Operations, GOM OCS Region.

Procedures   On 6 May 2002, MMS personnel visited the MP-255 "A" platform and viewed the parts of the crane package that remained on the platform after the accident. They examined the layout, weld residue, and general platform condition following the fall of the crane.

On 10 May 2002, the MMS investigation team visited the operating base of Devon Resources, hereinafter referred to as "Devon" or "Operator," in Boothville-Venice, La. The recovered wreckage of the crane was examined and three people were interviewed about the accident. These were the Devon company representative, the Island Operating Co. representative, and a Universal Cranes Company crane safety investigator under contract to Devon.

On 16 May 2002, personnel from the MMS New Orleans Regional Office visited the offices of Devon in Lafayette, La., and interviewed the Safety Manager, Devon, and the contract supervisor (company man) for the Operator during the construction. On 20 May 2002, two personnel from the MMS New Orleans Regional and District offices visited the offices of Devon in Lafayette, La., and interviewed six members of the construction work crew that witnessed the accident. All were employees of the Mar-Con, Inc., (hereinafter referred to as "Mar-Con" or "Contractor"). On 31 July 2002, MMS personnel interviewed three additional personnel from Mar-Con, who were the two Mar-Con crane supervisors who installed the crane and the Mar-Con Operations Manager.

In July 2002, MMS personnel obtained a copy of the Anderson Associates,

Consulting Metallurgical Engineers and Testing Laboratory, report *Metallurgical*

Investigation of a Fractured Crane Support Weld, *6/24/02* to help resolve the

cause of the failure of the crane. Additionally, to further the investigation, MMS

personnel gathered the following documents:

Mar-Con supervisor safety meeting report, 5/5/02, 6AM – list of attendees;
Crane certification for crane operator;
Devon Incident Report Form;
Mar-Con supervisor's report of accident;
Mar-Con accident investigation report;
Crane certificate of test, TC20, April 2002;
Crane certificate of test, TC20 May 2, 2002;
Mar-Con, Inc., Crane Inspection Requirements check list;
Welding Certification for welders;
Mar-con fabrication drawings for crane, 8/8/99;
Devon – Versabar rigging rental equipment contract and list;
SOCO Offshore, Technical Engineering Consultants, stack vent boom plan,
10/1/97.

Introduction

Background   Lease OCS-G 07825 covers approximately 5,000 acres and is located in Main

Pass Block 255, Gulf of Mexico, offshore, Louisiana. *(For lease location, see*

Attachment 1.) The lease is jointly owned by Devon SFS Operating, Inc.,

Newfield Exploration Co., TotalFinaElf E&P USA, Inc., and Piquant, Inc. The

lease was issued effective 1 August 1985, and Devon was last named designated

operator effective 12 April 2001.

Brief   On the morning of Sunday, 5 May 2002, construction operations were underway
Description of
the Accident   to install a new flare boom and to remove the old, 18,000-lb flare boom from

Devon's MP-255 "A" platform (*see Attachment 2*). The old flare boom was to be

removed from the platform's north side and lowered onto a work boat by using a

temporarily installed rental crane. The old flare boom was cut loose from the

platform and held by the rental crane. While the load was being swung around

the northeast corner of the platform, prior to lowering it onto the boat, the welded

base of one of the rental crane's two support braces failed. This caused the crane

suddenly to be uprooted from the platform and be pulled overboard into the Gulf

of Mexico. The movement of the crane overboard caused the death of one

crewmember who was in the path of the falling crane.

Findings

Chronology
of Events
1. Early spring, 2002 — A meeting of the Devon company-wide construction group was held to begin planning for removal of the old flare boom, installation of the new boom, and to reconfigure MP-255 "A" Platform piping.

2. March–April, 2002 — Planning meeting including Devon construction personnel, the contract construction supervisor for Devon, and Mar-Con personnel to plan procedures, timing, equipment, etc., for the proposed job.

The following dates and times are approximate, because of inconsistency in testimonies:

3. Monday, 29 April, 2002 — Load-out equipment, arrive at the platform and lift the crane and equipment onto platform.

4. Tuesday, 30 April, 2002 — Change procedure to install the crane only in one location. This new method and the associated operation procedure were developed and proposed by the crane supervisor (CS-1) in consultation with the contract company-man (CM), the Mar-Con construction supervisor (SC), and was the subject of a lengthy conversation between crane supervisor no. 1 (CS-1) and the Mar-Con operations manager (OM).

5. Tuesday, 30 April, 2002 — The crane was installed in a "second" location as per newly agreed methodology and procedure (*see Attachment 2*). Installation included use of "spacer" I-beam to form the base of one of the braces supporting the crane.

6. Wednesday, 1 May, 2002 — The crane was rigged up by CS-1, hooked to the old flare boom, and pull-tested to 26K. Several cables, swivel heads, etc., were found to be incorrectly rigged up. When it was found that the cables on the spool

5

were too short to accomplish the job, CS-1 was replaced by crane supervisor #2 (CS-2).

7. Thursday, 2 May, 2002 — CS-2 completed the rig up of the crane, pull-tested the crane to 30K while hooked to the old flare boom.

8. Friday, 3 May, 2002 — Installation of new flare boom accomplished per procedure proposed by CS-1, and agreed to by the SC, OM and CM. This involved a mid-air relay of the load between the platform crane and rental crane. The crew then finished the piping modifications and other tasks required to return the platform to production and prepare for the removal of the old flare boom.

9. At approximately 0600 hrs, Sunday, 5 May, 2002 — Safety meeting prior to removing old flare boom conducted by Mar-Con SC.

10. At approximately 0610 hrs, the crane operator (CO) positioned the crane control panel on the east rail of the platform to have maximum visibility while loading onto boat. The welder (W) is positioned next to the crane operator to watch the crane hydraulic hoses, keeping them from possibly being pinched or cut when the load was swung.

11. At approximately 0700 hrs, 5 May 2002, the CO, operating the rental crane, took bind on the old flare boom, and the old flare boom was cut free from the platform by the fitter (F).

12. At approximately 0730 hrs., the work boat backed under the load on the north side of the platform, and was warned off by the SC and CM. The CO began to boom the load down and around the northeast corner of the platform, preparing to load the old flare onto the boat on the east side of the platform.

13. At approximately 0800 hrs, as the rental crane boom holding the old flare swung around from roughly a heading of 0° (north) to approximately 50° (east-northeast) (*see Attachment 3*), the E-W crane brace pulled up from the deck.

6

Immediately, the rest of the crane was pulled from the welded supports and the N-S brace broke. The crane and load were pulled from the platform into the Gulf. W, watching the cables, was apparently entangled in the hoses, pulled into the guardrail of the platform, hit by the falling crane, and thrown 90 feet out into the Gulf.

14. At approximately 0820 hrs, two members of the crew donned life jackets, swam to the welder floating face down in the Gulf, and helped load him into the boat.

15. At approximately 1130 hrs., after W had been given 1½ hrs of resuscitation, med-evac personnel arrived and declared the welder deceased. He was taken by helicopter to the hospital.

Description of Proposed Procedures

In May, Devon planned to begin drilling operations on MP-255 "A" platform using a jack-up rig moved onto the platform's north side. To facilitate the drilling plans, Devon decided to remove a flare boom blocking rig access to the platform. They planned to install a new flare boom on the east side of the platform, re-pipe the production lines to access the new flare boom, and then remove the old flare boom from the north side of the platform. As the platform crane was located too far away to be able to stab the new flare boom or to remove the old flare boom, the Devon construction group planned to use a temporary rental crane installed on the platform to accomplish the tasks.

Contractor relationships — Devon employed a contract construction supervisor, the CM, to assist in the coordination of the planning of the operation and to act as the company representative during the actual operation. Devon then asked the

OM for Mar-Con, Inc., a supplier of offshore rental cranes and construction personnel, to propose a method of accomplishing the tasks.

The Mar-Con offshore construction division provided the work crews and the SC to conduct the actual operations, including installing the new flare boom, removing the old flare boom, and reconfiguring the platform piping to the new flare boom. The Mar-Con offshore crane division supplied a crane supervisor (CS-1 and CS-2) to oversee the installation and rigging up of the rental crane. The Mar-Con CS-1, CS-2, and SC reported to the Mar-Con OM. The Devon construction CM reported to the Devon construction superintendent located in Houston. Apparently, the Operator discourages its CM's from directly interfering in the technical aspects of a specialty construction job, such as setting up a crane. Devon prefers to rely on the expertise of the contractor in such cases unless a clear and obvious fault requires CM intervention.

Planning for operation(s) — At a meeting in early spring, representatives of Mar-Con met with Devon personnel, including the CM, and discussed the various alternatives available for accomplishing the job, including alternatives proposing to use a 100-ton crane or a 40-ton crane. It was found that the two large cranes would be difficult to set up in the restricted space of the platform. However, the Mar-Con personnel proposed an alternative, using a 20-ton crane set up in two separate locations, the first to lift and stab the new flare boom, and the second to help remove the old flare boom (*see Attachment 2*). This plan was accepted and the CM, acting as Devon's project coordinator, requested the job be "fully engineered." It was agreed that Mar-Con was to supply contract construction personnel to install the rental crane, construct the platform piping reconfiguration, install the new flare boom, and remove the old flare boom.

Though Devon construction personnel used a contract engineering company to determine the weight of the old flare boom, they did not develop a written procedure for the various portions of the operation to be conducted by Mar-Con personnel. Devon also did not require a written procedure to be developed by Mar-Con. Other than a platform plat showing the two installation locations for the rental crane, no written procedure was supplied by Mar-Con either to Devon or to its own employees showing how to install the crane on the platform or conduct the operation.

A verbal discussion of the procedure(s) between the OM and CM sufficed for a plan of operations to accomplish the various tasks. The Mar-Con OM previously had instructed his personnel, and thought it was implicitly understood by Mar-Con employees that company policy required any change from "standard" crane installation methodology or job procedure to be cleared with the Mar-Con OM. However, there was no written definition of what was regarded as standard installation methodology.

Installation of Crane and Initial Activities

On approximately 29 April 2002, the Mar-Con crew moved on location. The construction crew was supervised by the SC and CS-1, who was on site to oversee the installation and rig-up of the crane. The CM was also on site. The CM, SC, and CS-1 reviewed the plans for the job and concluded that the intended procedure, which envisioned setting the crane in two separate locations, could be revised in such a way as to allow the crane to be set only once, in the second location (*see Attachment 2*). This new plan was made possible by using the platform crane in conjunction with the rental crane to perform the first lift, the setting of the new flare boom. The new plan used the two cranes in tandem to transfer the load from one to the other in mid-air. This new procedure was the subject of a lengthy conversation between the CS-1 and OM.

After the new procedure was agreed upon by all parties, the construction crew, supervised by CS-1, set up the crane (*see Attachment 4*). The dimensions and spacing needed to allow the pad-eye base of the two crane support braces (N-S and E-W) to be welded directly onto the platform support beams were measured to determine the location for the king post. The king post was then welded down to the deck and the N-S brace was welded, its pad-eye base being set directly on a support beam as planned. It was then discovered the E-W brace pad-eye overlapped the main skid beam, which was supposed to be its weld point, by about 6 inches (*see Attachment 5*).

When it was discovered that the E-W brace pad-eye could not be directly welded to the main skid beam, the CS-1 opted to install the crane in a different manner. Instead of taking up the king-post and N-S brace pad-eye and resetting them so that the E-W brace pad-eye would fall on the skid beam, the crane supervisor used a ? x 10-inch I-beam (taken from the tool basket) to create a base for the E-W brace. This I-beam was first attached to the skid beam by four 8-inch fillet welds, and then the pad-eye of the E-W brace was welded to the I-beam. The ends of the I-beam were unsupported (*see diagram, Attachment 5; picture Attachment 6*). In a conversation between the CS-1 and the OM that day, no mention of this method of setting up the crane was made, that conversation being exclusively concerned with the change in procedure for setting the new flare boom.

This method of setting the crane brace created a cantilever, with the I-beam/E-W brace pad-eye connection being outboard of the I-beam/skid beam welds. This situation allowed a force moment, multiplying the force applied to the I-beam/pad eye connection onto the I-beam/skid beam connection. The I-beam itself had been used as a base for a crane brace several times and was previously modified by the removal of about 22 inches of the bottom flange (*see Attachment 7*). The method previously used was to weld the I-beam onto two or three support beams, thus providing a more stable base than the cantilever employed in this application.

Following the installation of the crane, the CM asked CS-1 about the soundness of the method employed to set the crane using a cantilever I-beam. He was told by CS-1 that the method was used "all the time." CM also asked if CS-1 had spoken to the OM, and was told that CS-1 had indeed talked to OM. Then, the CS-1 rigged-up the crane, spooled the cables, and the crane was attached to the old flare boom and reportedly pull-tested to 26 Klbs.

The next morning the crew prepared to lift and install the new flare boom using the mid-air transfer in conjunction with the platform crane. When the rental crane was rotated into position for the job, the top sheave assembly flipped and the cables twisted 180°. After the cables were untwisted, the block was respooled and lowered to the water, and it was discovered that the cables were 60 ft. too short for the job. Other problems with the spooling of the cables, etc., then became evident. At that time, CM informed OM that he wished to replace CS-1. CS-2 was sent to the platform and CS-1 was sent in.

The following morning, CS-2 arrived with the new spool of cable for the crane. He respooled and rigged up the crane, reassembled the crane, and fixed the twisted cables. He then reportedly pull-tested the crane to 30 Klbs with the crane in the same test position as before, attached to the old flare boom in line (180°) with the N-S brace (*see Attachment 2*). CS-2 looked over the crane setup and noticed the cantilever beam support of the E-W brace was unusual, but as spacer I-beams were occasionally used (though not in this manner), he assumed it had been approved by the OM. After the pull test, the crane was declared ready for the lift. That evening, the new flare boom was lifted onto the platform by the platform crane and the following day was successfully stabbed into place using the mid-air load transfer procedure. CS-2 departed the platform.

Attempted Removal of Old Flare Boom and Accident

At 6:00 AM Sunday, 5 May 2002, the piping connections having been completed, the last remaining operation was removal of the old flare boom. In a safety meeting with the crew, the SC assigned roles, discussed dangers, pinch points, and discussed procedures. The crane operator (CO) positioned the movable control panel on the east side of the platform because he believed he could better see the entire operation. A welder (W) was assigned to ensure no hoses were caught in the operating mechanism of the crane during the operation. (*See Attachment 8 for example of typical hydraulic hoses and Attachment 3 for diagram of personnel location and platform geography.*) It was felt necessary to have a crew member watch the hoses because one had once been pinched as the crane was swung. The crewmember (W) took his position next to the hoses.

However, he was positioned in such a manner that he was inside the potential danger zone should the crane fall. No written JSA or JHA addressed the danger of standing in that position and no supervisors corrected the position of W.

Once it was cut free, the CO planned to swing the load around the northeast corner of the platform and lower it onto the boat. The CO set the agenda for lowering the load onto the boat on the east side of the platform. Though the CM and SC had previously assumed it would be dropped straight down from its position on the north side of the platform, no procedure had been written requiring this course of action.

The fitter (F), who was to cut off the flare boom, tied off his safety line (on the guard rail), cut the bottom, east and then west legs, and the flare boom was held by the crane. (Note: The flare is positioned in line with the N-S brace). After 20 min, the operator prepared to swing the load around the northeast corner (*see Attachment 3*). The boat came in under the load prematurely and only after much verbal warning by the CM and SC was the boat induced to get out of the way. The CO lowered the load slightly, began to swing the load around the corner while verbally reciting the angles, load etc., readings from his gauges. When the load "broke the corner," (i.e., the boom pointed to the east of northeast corner of the platform or at an angle of about 50° from the initial boom alignment (*see Attachment 3*), two loud snaps were heard. The E-W brace and pad eye connection, including the I-beam, was seen to "pop up," torn loose from the skid beam. The crane and load then disappeared into the Gulf of Mexico. The W, who was watching the hoses, was seen entangled in hoses. He was pulled into the guardrail by the hoses and the crane itself, and then was spun out over the

13

side into the Gulf. (*See Attachment 9, picture of platform location of crane after accident.*)

Calls were placed to the Coast Guard to initiate a search, as it was thought that several men were in the water. A med-evac was also summoned. The CM organized a head-count, which confirmed that only one man, W, was in the water and the Coast Guard search was later canceled. Two men ran to the +10 deck, donned lifejackets, and went into the Gulf to rescue the W, who was floating face down. With some difficulty, the two men in the water pulled him onto the work boat with assistance from the deckhands on the boat. Life support resuscitation was given and the victim was lifted onto the platform in a personnel basket. Life support respiration continued to be administered until the arrival of the med evac, one hour later, at which time the victim was pronounced dead. He was taken to the hospital.

Post-accident Investigation Activities On 7 May 2002, the crane was recovered from the Gulf of Mexico and transported to Island Operating Company base in Boothville-Venice, La. At that location, on 10 May, members of the MMS investigation team, with personnel representing the Operator, inspected the crane.

The inspection revealed that the I-beam that formed the base for the E-W brace had deformed considerably where the beam was welded to the skid beam of the platform. Portions of the beam flange had deformed and chunks of the flange metal were apparently missing where it had been welded. (*See Attachment 10, fillet welds, and Attachment 11, picture of beam and deformation.*) The N-S brace had been broken above the pad eye connection to the platform structure,

14

with the pad eye connection remaining welded to the platform (*see Attachment 9*). The E-W brace had been bent but was intact. With the concurrence of the investigation team, the I-beam and the portion of the skid beam to which the I-beam had been welded, and all pad eye elements, were sent to Anderson & Associates, Consulting Metallurgical Engineers and Testing Laboratory, in Houston, to determine the failure mechanism.

Four groups of witnesses to the accident, management, supervisors, and policy personnel were interviewed to develop a chronology of events leading up to the accident. The training and expertise of the principals in the incident were also examined and questioned during the interviews and through the acquisition of documents, plats, etc. The Contractor and Operator management and supervisory personnel were interviewed to develop the methodology and procedures planned and employed in the conduct of the operation. Extensive photographic evidence was developed to corroborate the physical geography related to the incident.

Analysis of Crane Structural Failure   On 17 June, a complete report on the metallurgy investigation of the failed portion of the crane base was received from Anderson & Associates. That Anderson investigation concluded that the attachment of the E-W crane brace to the platform failed when the boom was rotated to the point where that brace took most of the load.

The report noted the I-beam that formed the connection between the E-W brace pad-eye and the platform was placed across the skid beam with the ends of the I-beam hovering in the air, unsupported, forming a cantilever. The bottom flange of the I-beam was attached to the skid beam using four fillet welds. The four fillet welds failed *(see Attachment 10)*. The report noted there was significant deformation of the bottom flange of the I-beam and all such deformation was precisely oriented around the welds *(see Attachments 11, 12, and 13)*.

The report stated that it was discovered the materials involved in the failure were basically sound. The I-beam and skid beam were proper structural grade steels and the welds were properly made. The weld fusion was good, the weld was stronger than the metals it attached, and the weld size could not have been any larger because it was limited by the thickness of the I-beam flange. The report concluded the failure of the brace support was completely caused by an overload on the I-beam. The degree of bending of the I-beam flange was such that the fillet welds became loaded more in tension than in shear and the beam itself then failed. The report noted that the failure of the crane brace that led to the accident was caused by the incorrect fundamental design of the attachment of the crane to the platform.

Additional extensive interviews with the principals of the Operator and Contractor and the witnesses, and examination of the documents previously provided, produced consensus conclusions by the panel.

Conclusions

The Accident After a review of the information obtained during the course of this investigation, it is the conclusion of this panel that on the morning of 5 May 2002, construction operations were underway to install a new flare boom and to remove the old flare boom from Devon's MP-255 "A" platform. The old flare boom was cut loose from the platform and held by the rental crane. While the load was being swung to begin lowering it onto the boat, the base of the E-W brace attaching the crane to the platform failed, causing the crane suddenly to be uprooted from the platform and be pulled overboard into the Gulf of Mexico. The movement of the crane overboard caused the death of a crewmember who was in the path of the falling crane.

Cause 1. The failure of the crane brace was directly caused by a fault in the fundamental design of the way the crane was attached to the platform. The method of attaching the E-W crane brace to the skid beam using a cantilevered I-beam was insufficient to withstand the force applied in the course of the operation.

2. The deficient fundamental design was used because of organizational failures as follows:

- No engineering calculations were required or employed by the Operator or Contractor to ensure the adequacy of the attachment design;
- No written procedure for installing the crane was required or employed by the Operator or Contractor to ensure competent review of field modifications of standard installation procedures.

17

3. No written Joint Safety Analysis (JSA)/Job Hazard Analysis (JHA) was required or created by the Operator or Contractor. A written JSA of the operation could reasonably have been expected to have identified the hazard of positioning a crewmember within a zone that would place him at risk in the event of a crane failure.

4. The load testing of the crane prior to conducting the operation did not reveal the structural flaws of the installation, indicating that the standards for testing cranes of this type do not provide a true indication of the ability of this type of crane to perform safely the full range of motion required to complete a job.

Contributing Causes

1. Contributing to the fatal accident was the lack of a formal, written procedure provided by the Contractor or Operator that defined the steps and checkpoints of the construction job as a whole.

2. The CM, SC, CS-1, and CS-2 overseeing the operation failed to recognize the structural deficiency of the installation. CS-1, who installed the crane, failed to recognize that the cantilever method of using an I-beam as the base for the E-W brace was significantly different from other methods of using an I-beam as a base. This may have caused his failure to discuss and review the installation method with the OM.

Possible Contributing Causes

Possibly contributing to the accident were the following:

1. Verbal communication misunderstandings – The CM asked the CS-1 if he had "talked to the OM," apparently meaning to inquire if the CS-1 had reviewed the

mechanics of the crane setup with the OM. The CS-1 had replied that he had "talked to the OM." But, though he had talked to the OM, he had talked exclusively about the change in procedure for the first lift, not the crane setup. As a result, the CM assumed that the experienced OM had endorsed the crane setup. However, the OM later said that the actual setup was completely abnormal and should have been reviewed by him, but that the subject was not raised by CS-1.

2. The failure of the CS-1 to review the setup with the OM was possibly caused by the lack of explicit written Contractor guidelines defining under what circumstances the setup of a crane will be reviewed by the OM. The Operator also did not require written guidelines to be provided or used to perform any part of the operation.

3. The failure by the CM to reject the setup of the crane was possibly caused by a lack of definition by the Operator of the role of the CM. Apparently, the Operator has a policy allowing the Contractor to have control over the technical aspects of a construction job. The Operator appears to discourage their CM from intervening in the operational aspects of a job involving a contractor unless there is a clear and present problem. No written job description defines the role of the contracted CM.

Recommendations

Safety Alert   The Gulf of Mexico OCS Region should issue a Safety Alert to read as follows:

Recently, an operator hired a construction/rental crane contractor to remove an 18,000 lbs. flare boom from a platform. The rental crane was installed and the old flare boom was cut lose. During the swinging of the load to begin lowering it onto the boat, the base of the E-W brace attaching the rental crane to the platform failed. This caused the crane to be torn suddenly from the platform and pulled overboard into the Gulf of Mexico. The movement of the crane overboard caused the death of a crewmember who was in the path of the falling crane.

Cause   1. The failure of the crane brace was directly caused by a fault in the fundamental design of the way the crane was attached to the platform. The crane was held in place by two braces welded to the platform, one oriented E-W and one N-S. When attaching the E-W crane brace to the platform, the contractor first welded the brace to a small I-beam. Then, the I-beam was welded to the platform skid beam in such a manner that the I-beam/brace attachment was outboard of the I-beam/skid beam weld and the I-beam ends were unsupported. This created a cantilever effect that multiplied the forces on the I-beam to the point that the I-beam failed when exposed to the full load of the lift.

2. The deficient fundamental design was allowed because of organizational failures as follows:

- No engineering calculations were required or employed by the Operator or Contractor to ensure the adequacy of the attachment design;

- No written procedure for installing the crane was required or employed by the Operator or Contractor to ensure competent review of field modifications of standard installation procedures.

3. No written JSA/JHA was required or created by the Operator or Contractor. A JSA analysis of the operation could reasonably have been expected to have identified the hazard of positioning a crewmember within a zone that would place him at risk in the event of a crane failure.

4. The load testing of the crane prior to conducting the operation did not reveal the structural flaws of the installation. This failure indicates the standard method for load testing cranes of this type with the boom oriented only in one direction does not provide a true indication of the ability of the crane to perform safely the full range of motion required to complete a job.

5. The supervisors overseeing the operation failed to recognize the structural deficiency of the installation. The supervisor installing the crane failed to recognize that the cantilever method of using an I-beam as the base for the E-W brace was significantly different from other methods of using an I-beam as a connector. This likely caused a failure to discuss and review the installation method with company management.

Possible Contributions to the Failure

6. Possibly contributing to the fatal accident was the lack of a formal, written procedure provided by the Contractor or Operator that defined the steps and checkpoints of the construction job as a whole.

7. Verbal communication misunderstandings between the supervisors and on-shore management also possibly contributed to the accident.

Recommendations to Operators

The MMS recommends to the operators that they thoroughly review the engineering of attaching any rental crane to a structure. The MMS also recommends to the operators that they thoroughly prepare a written procedure that defines the circumstances requiring supervisor, management or engineering review of operations during the course of construction activities. The MMS recommends that formal JSA/JHA's be employed to identify risks to personnel prior to major construction activities.

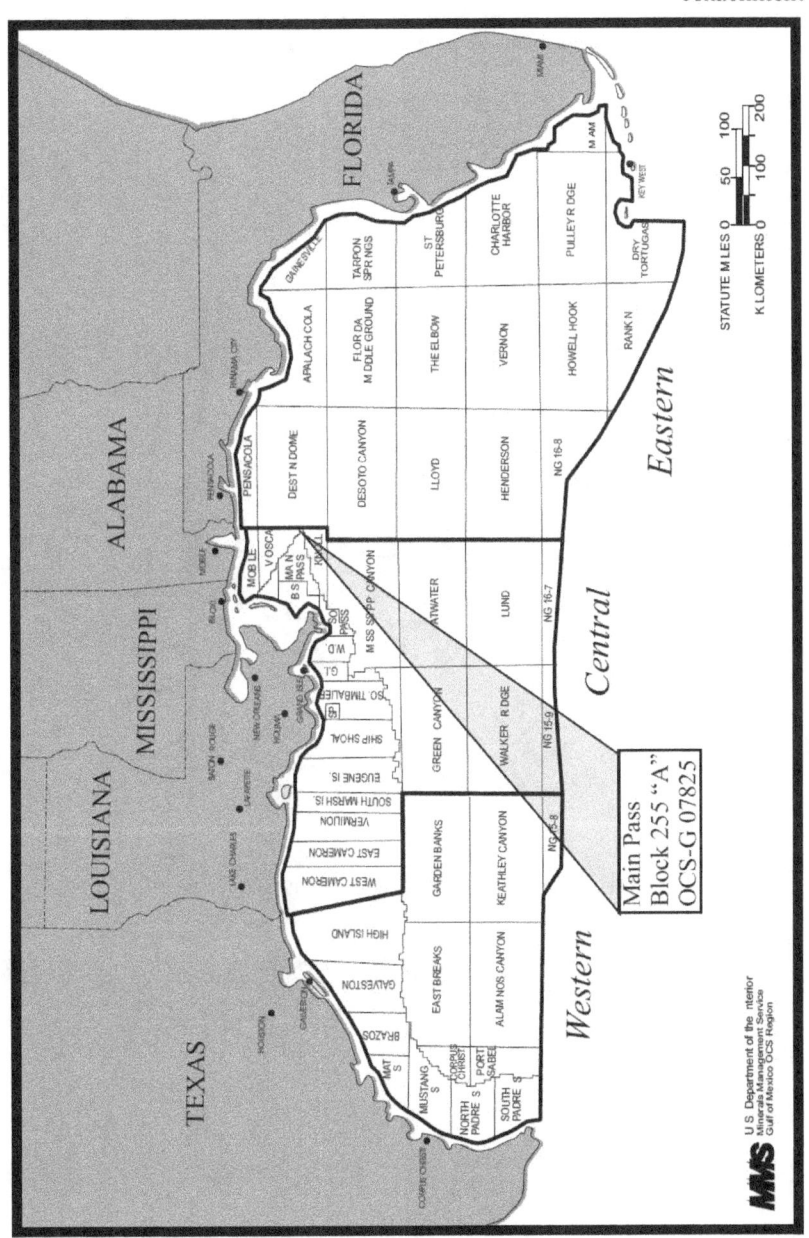

Location of Lease OCS-G 07825, Main Pass Block 255 "A"

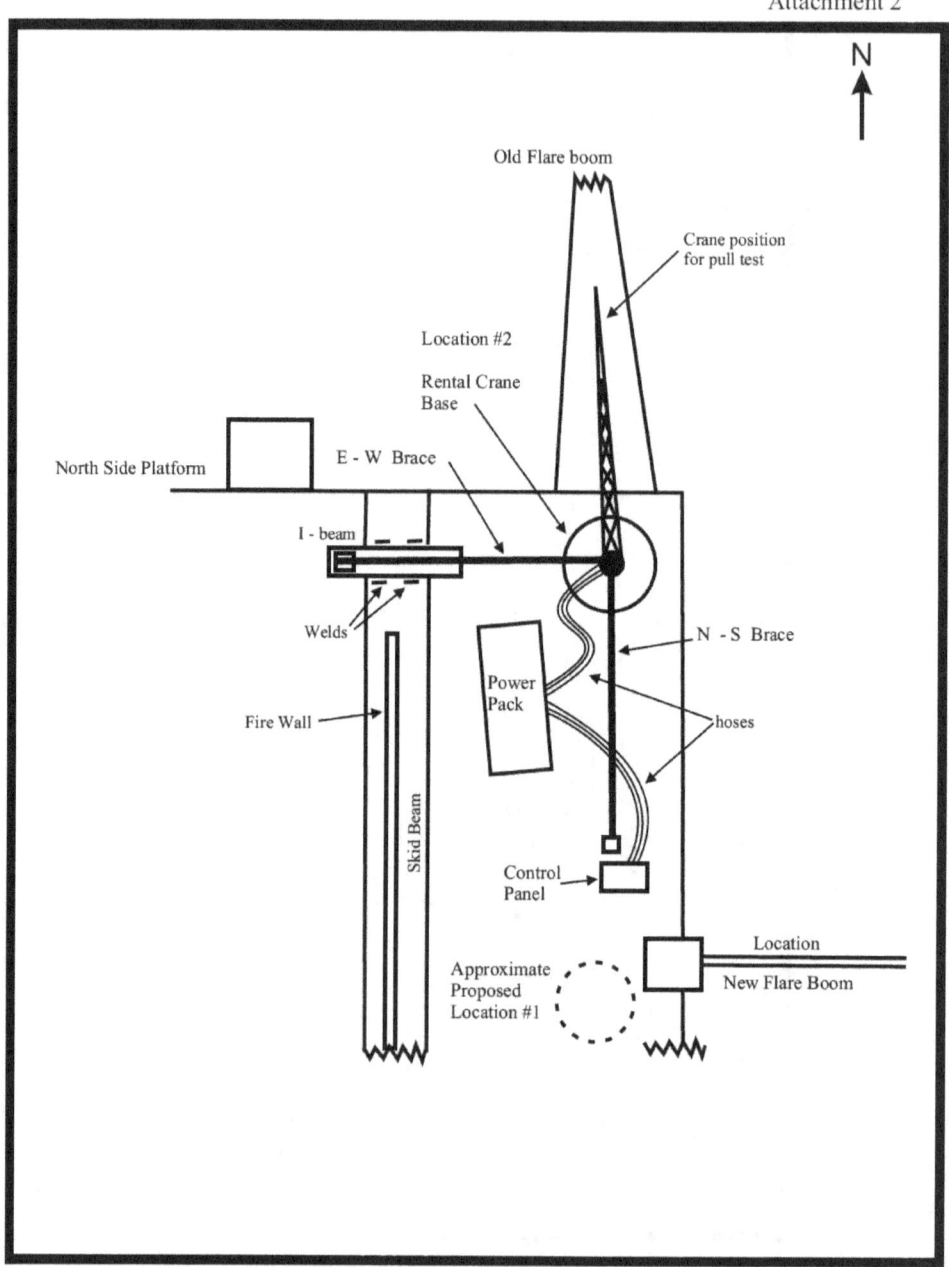

Diagram: Portion of Main Pass 255 "A" Platform with Rental Crane Positions.

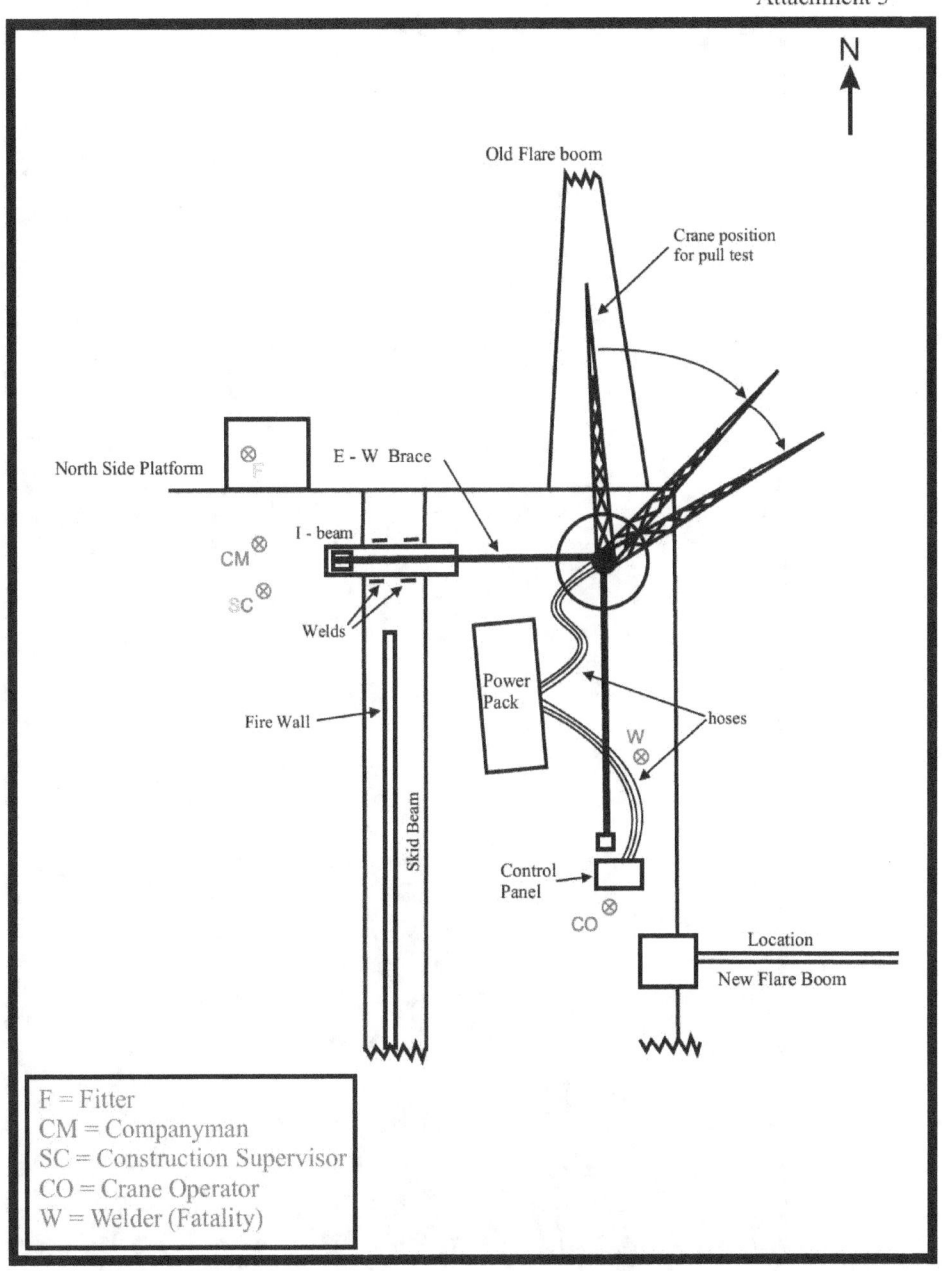

Old Flare boom

Crane position
for pull test

North Side Platform

E - W Brace

I - beam

CM

SC

Welds

Fire Wall

Skid Beam

Power
Pack

hoses

W

Control
Panel

CO

Location

New Flare Boom

F = Fitter
CM = Companyman
SC = Construction Supervisor
CO = Crane Operator
W = Welder (Fatality)

Diagram: Personnel Locations and Rental Crane Swing Path with/Load.

Braces
Welding Braces to Platform

Typical Installation of Rental Crane (Not MP - 255 "A")

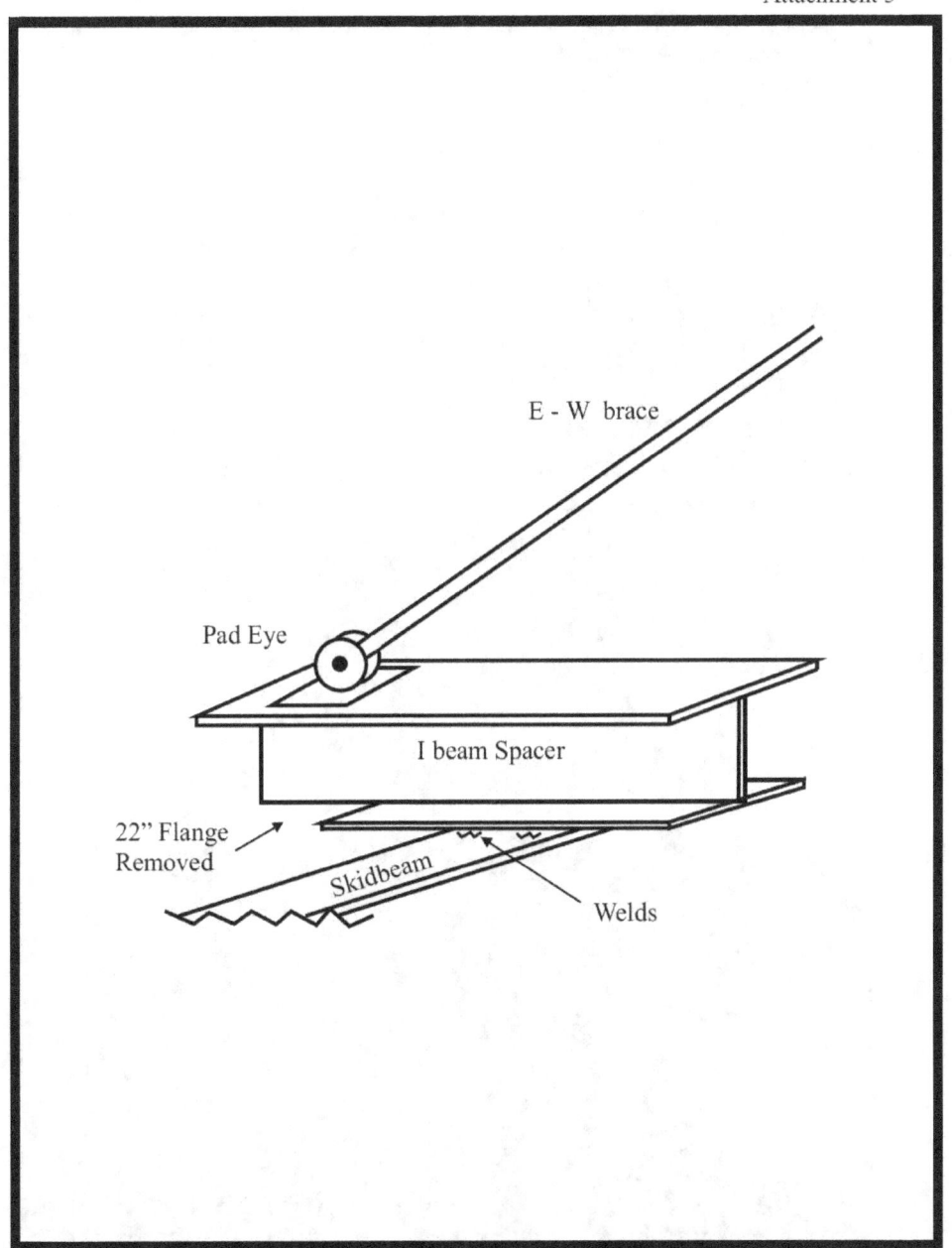

Diagram: Connection of Rental Crane E - W Brace to MP - 255 "A" Platform Skid Beam

I-Beam, Pad Eye w/Representation of Attachment to Skid Beam

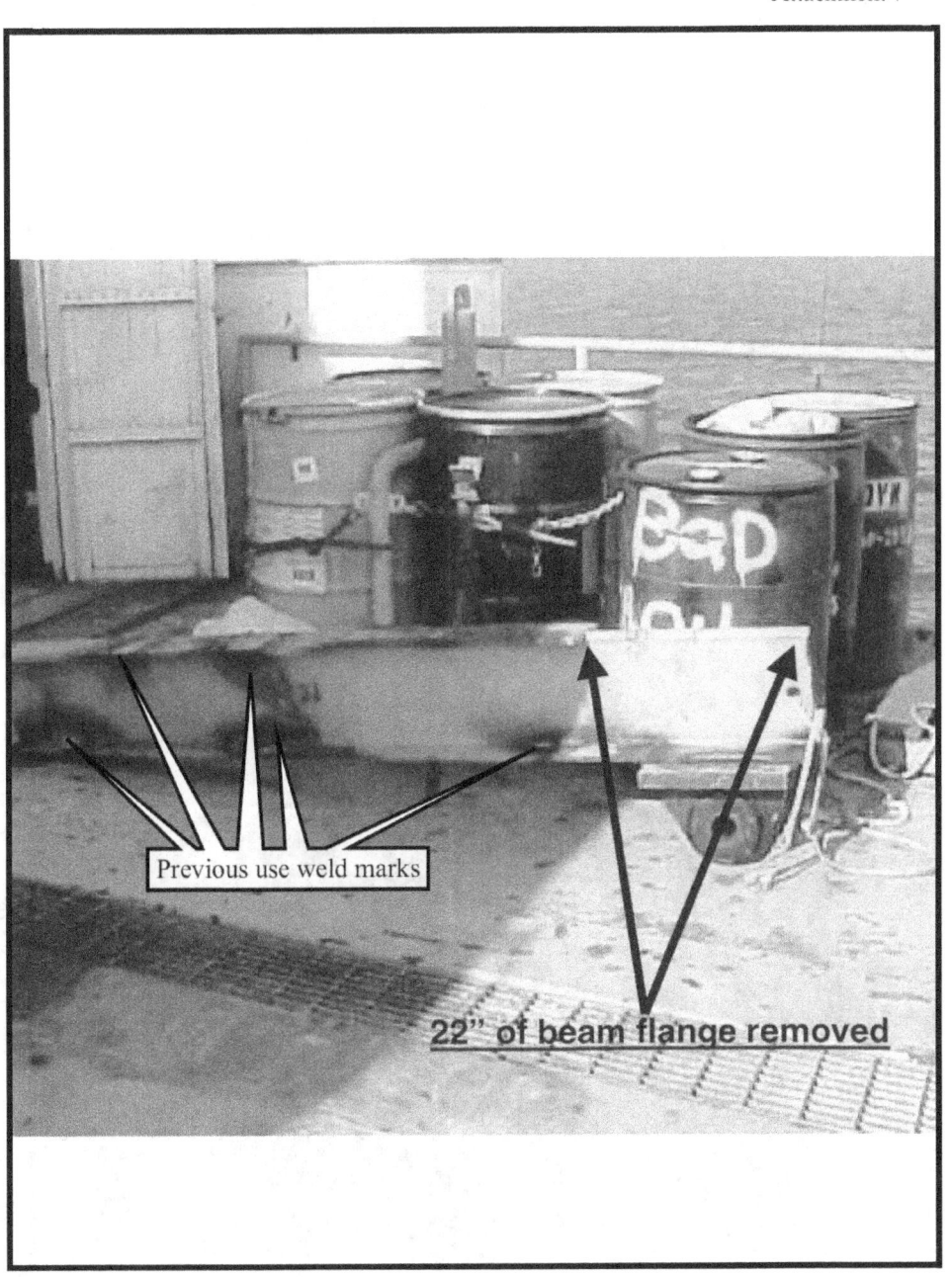

Previous use weld marks

22" of beam flange removed

I-Beam with Missing Flange and Previous Use Weld Marks

Typical Installation (not MP-255 "A") with Hydraulic Hoses

Platform Location of Crane after Failure

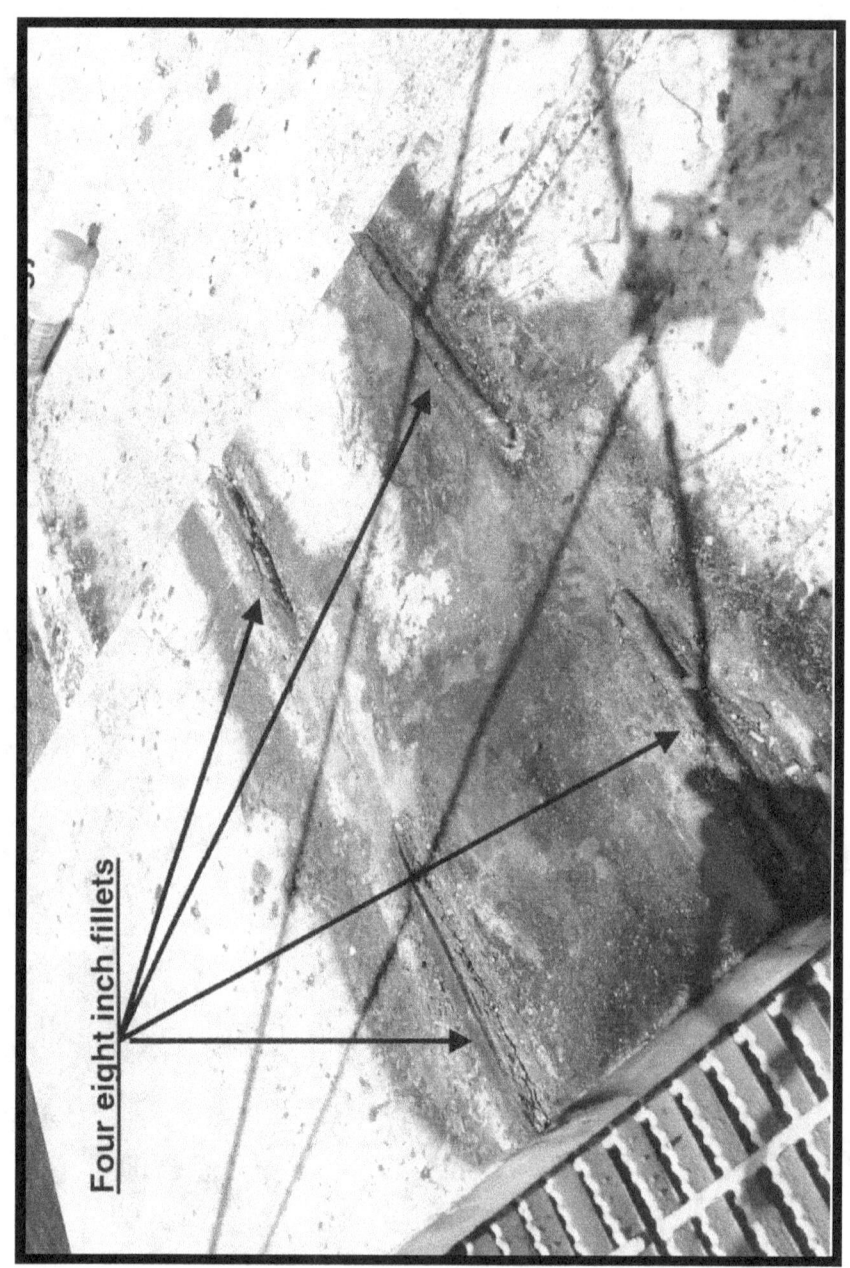

Four eight inch fillets

Fillet weld on skid beam after failure

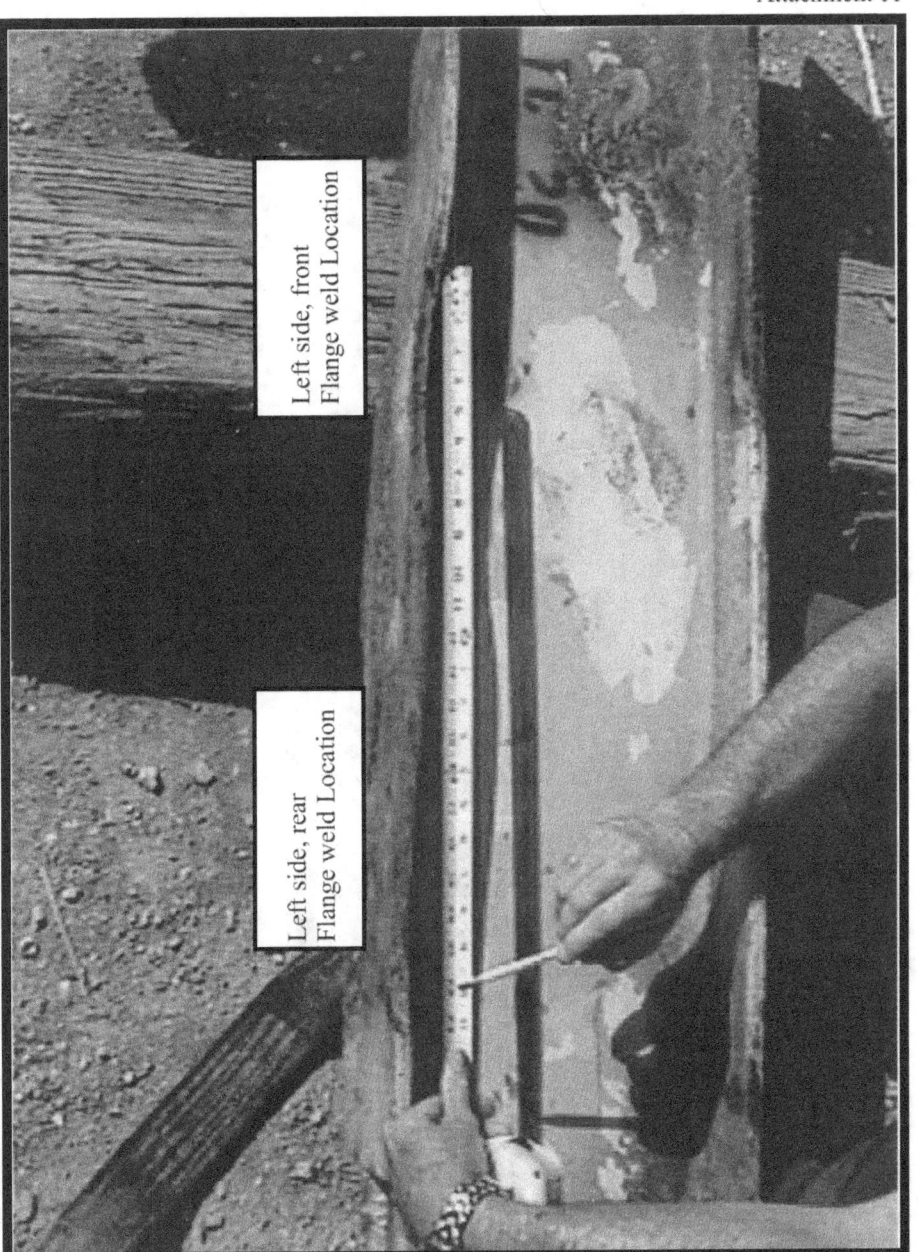

Left side, front
Flange weld Location

Left side, rear
Flange weld Location

Deformation of I-Beam Flange

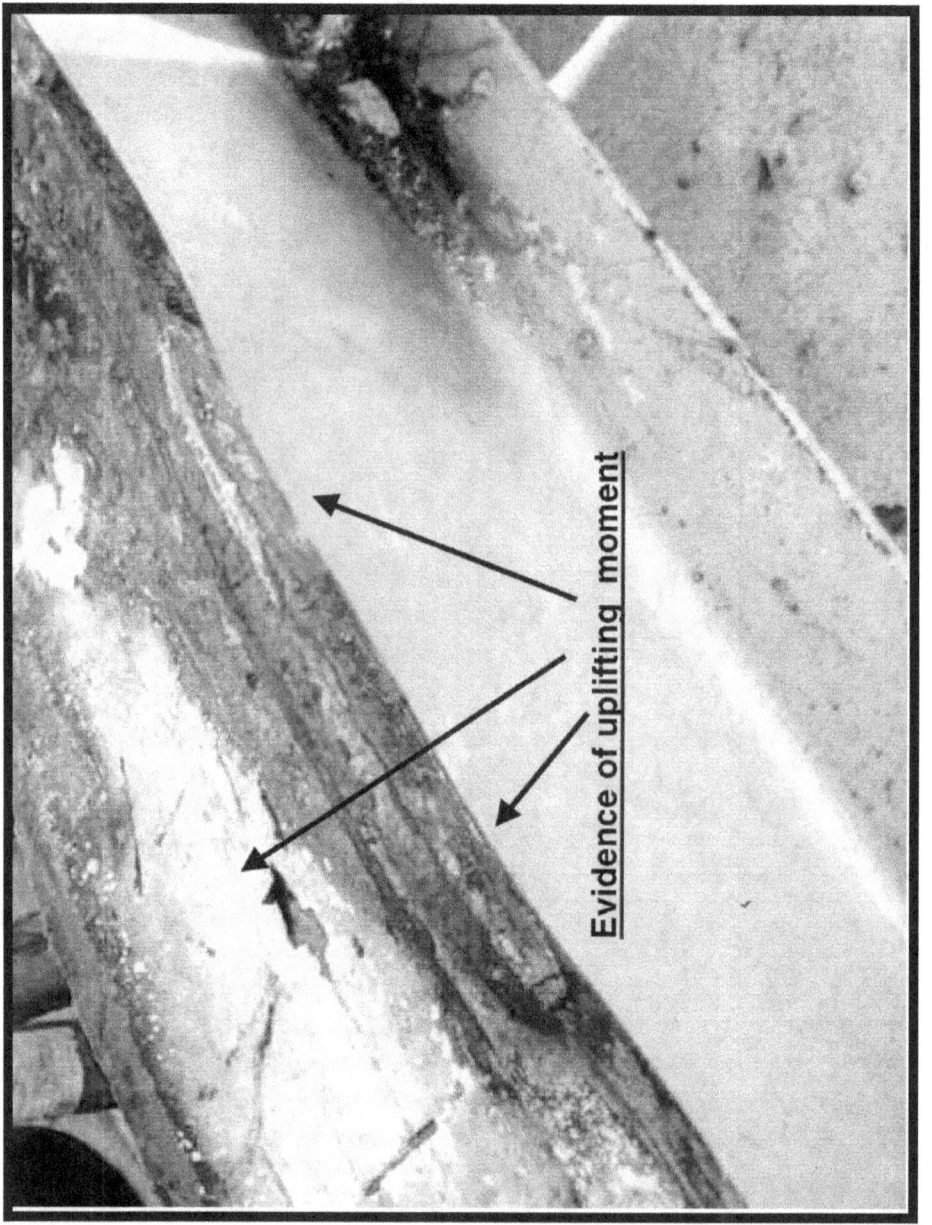

I-Beam Evidence of uplifting moment

I-Beam Flange Deformation after Failure